THE BIGGEST, SMALLEST, FASTEST, TALLEST

Things You've Ever Heard Of

WRITTEN AND ILLUSTRATED BY

Robert Lopshire

Thomas Y. Crowell   New York

To Selma and Marilyn,
who helped me get it all together.

What is the tallest building in the world?

The Sears Tower in Chicago, Illinois.
It is fourteen hundred and fifty-four
feet high.

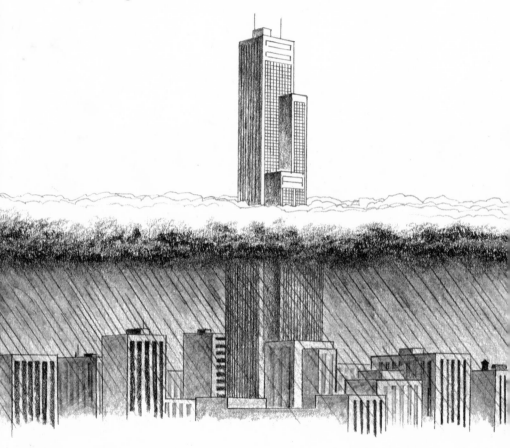

The second tallest buildings are
the two towers of the World Trade Center
in New York City.

What is the longest river in the world?

The Amazon River in South America.
It is over four thousand miles long.

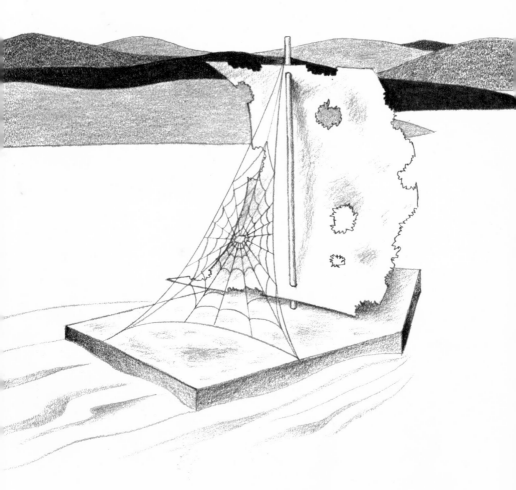

Some people say the Nile River in Egypt
is the longest river in the world.
It depends on how you measure them.

What is the biggest animal in the world?

The blue whale.

It can be over one hundred feet long,
and weigh as much as thirty elephants.

When it is born, a baby blue whale
is bigger than a small truck.

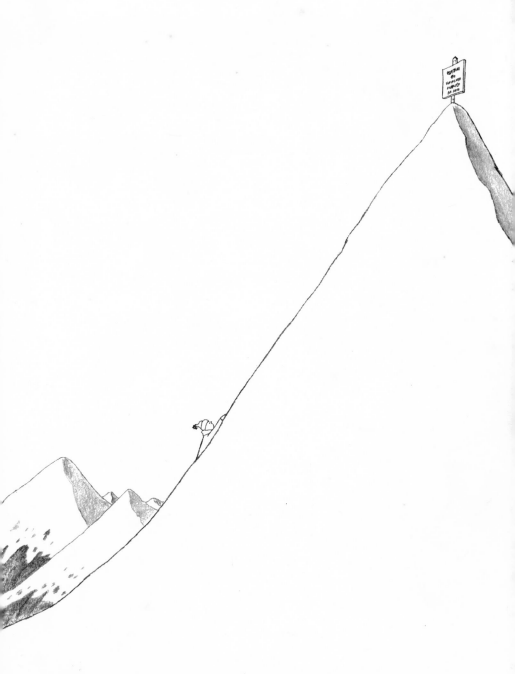

What is the highest mountain in the world?

Mount Everest, between Tibet and Nepal.
It is over five miles high.
What a great place to take a sled!

The largest canyon in the world
is the Grand Canyon in Arizona.
It is over two hundred miles long.

What is the biggest house in the world?

The Biltmore House in North Carolina.

It has two hundred and fifty rooms.

You could get lost in a place like that!

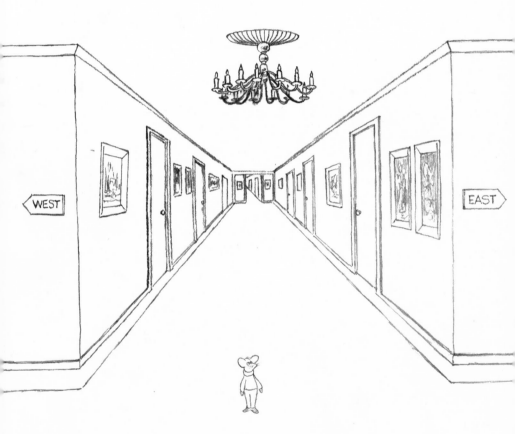

The biggest hotel in the world

is in Moscow, in the Soviet Union.

It has three thousand, two hundred rooms.

What is the tallest tree in the world?

The redwood tree.
Some redwoods grow
to be over three hundred
and fifty feet tall.

The tallest cactus in the world is
the saguaro. It can grow to be
over fifty feet tall.

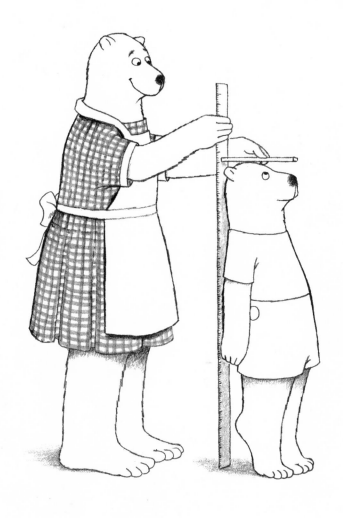

What is the tallest animal in the world?

The giraffe.
It can grow
to be almost
twenty feet tall!

When a baby giraffe
is born, it is
almost six feet tall.

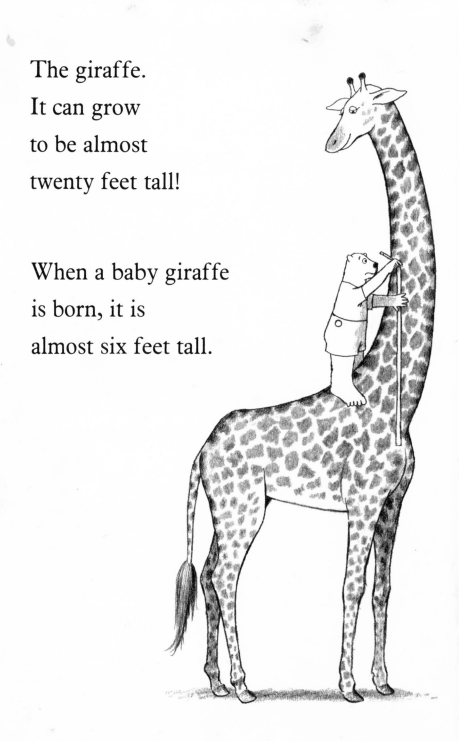

What is the biggest country in the world?

The Soviet Union is the biggest country.
It is more than twice as big
as the United States. That's big!

The country with the most people in it
is the People's Republic of China.
More than nine hundred million
people live there!

What place in the world
has the longest name?

A hill in New Zealand.
I'll bet you can't say its name.

A town in France has a very short name.
It is called Y.

What frog can jump the farthest?

The bullfrog can jump over you
and three of your friends.

A female bullfrog lays up to
twenty-five thousand eggs at a time.

What animal can run the fastest?

The cheetah.

It can run over sixty miles an hour.

The fastest animal in the world is
a bird called the spine-tailed swift. It
can fly over one hundred miles an hour.

What is the biggest dog in the world?

Don't let a Saint Bernard sit
in your lap. It can weigh over
two hundred and fifty pounds!

The smallest dog is the Chihuahua.
You can hold one in your hands...
if it will let you.

How big can fleas be?

Tell your dog to stay close to home!
Fleas in Washington State can be
as big as the end of your finger.

Fleas cannot fly. But they can
jump a very long way.

What was the heaviest dinosaur
that ever lived?

Brachiosaurus was probably the heaviest
dinosaur that ever lived. People think
it weighed more than seventeen elephants.

Luckily for us, the last one died
over a hundred million years ago!

What bird lays the biggest eggs?

The ostrich.

One egg weighs about four pounds, and is as big as your head.

The hummingbird lays the smallest eggs. Each egg is smaller than a jelly bean.

When you talk, what word
do you say the most?

You must like yourself very much!
You say "I" more than any other word.

When writing, people use the word *the*
more than any other word.

What is the biggest number of words
a parrot can learn?

A parrot in England
knows almost a thousand words.
It can ask for more than a cracker!

The heaviest bird in the world is
the ostrich. It can weigh as much as
three hundred and forty-five pounds.

What song is sung more than any other?

"Happy Birthday to You" is probably sung more often than any other song.

The second most often sung song is "For He's a Jolly Good Fellow."

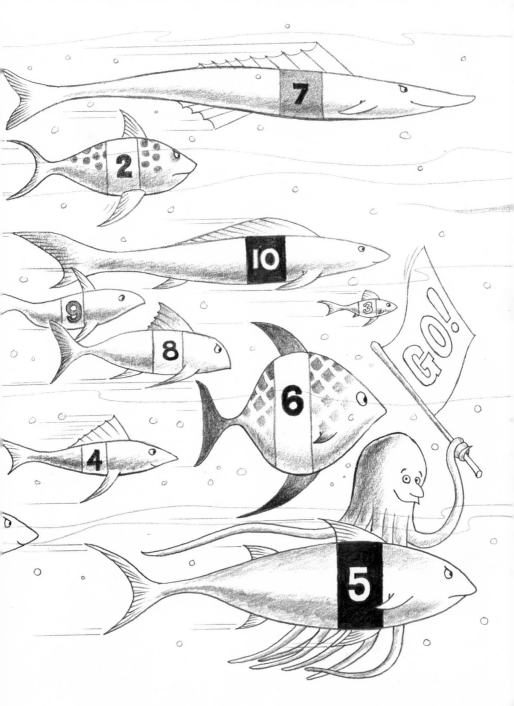

What is the fastest fish in the world?

The sailfish. It can swim
almost seventy miles an hour!

The fastest any person has been able
to swim is about five miles an hour.

What mammal has the most children?

A pig can have as many as
thirty-four babies at one time.
That's a lot of diapers to change!

Elephants have only one baby at a time,
but it can weigh two hundred pounds!
It needs a very big diaper.

Jones is a short last name.

Can you think of a shorter one?

Some people in Belgium
have a very short last name. It is O.
Their children have no trouble
learning to spell it.

A man in the United States has a name
so long it would not fit on this page.
It has almost six hundred letters in it.

What is the biggest cat in the world?

Be nice to this kitty!

A Siberian tiger can be as big as a car.

A tiger can eat up to fifty pounds
of meat in one day.

What animal has the biggest eyes?

The giant squid.

Its eyes are bigger than a dinner plate.

The giant squid has a very sharp beak.

It can bite through heavy wire!

How long was the longest worm ever found?

It was almost two hundred feet long,
longer than four buses!
It was a bootlace worm.

Don't go digging for bootlace worms.
They live only in the ocean.

What is the smallest bird in the world?

The hummingbird.

One kind of hummingbird
weighs less than a dime.
Hummingbirds can fly sideways
and even backwards!

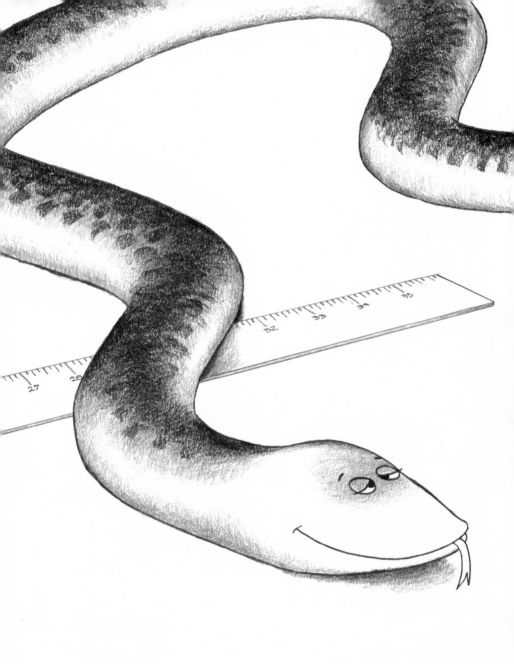

What is the longest snake in the world?

The anaconda.

It's longer than four beds. But don't worry. It sleeps in South America.

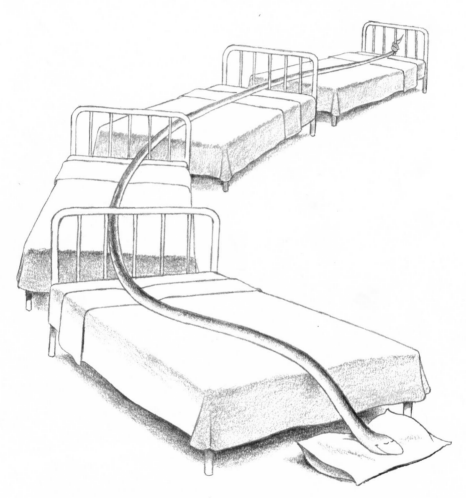

The shortest of all snakes is the thread snake. It's about as long as your hand.

What is the coldest it's
ever been in the world?

In Vostok, near the South Pole,
the temperature once got to be
126° below zero. Brrr.

In a town in Libya, a country in Africa,
the temperature once got as high as
136° above zero. That's hot!

How small do you think a horse can be?

The smallest horses in the world come from South America. Their shoulders are only fifteen inches from the ground.

The biggest horses in the world can weigh more than some cars.

What bird builds the biggest nest?

The bald eagle. It uses branches to build nests as tall as two-story houses.

Some hummingbirds build their nests with moss and spider webs.
These nests are smaller than your hand.

How many pages were there in the
longest book ever written?

I do not know.

But this book has sixty-four pages.

And now you've read them all!